CORGI BOOKS

THE GOLDEN RULES OF RUGBY

A CORGI BOOK 0 552 12591 1

First publication in Great Britain

PRINTING HISTORY
Corgi edition published 1985
Corgi edition reissued 1985

Corgi Books are published by Transworld Publishers Ltd.,
Century House, 61-63 Uxbridge Road, Ealing, London W5 5SA,
in Australia by Transworld Publishers (Aust.) Pty. Ltd.,
26 Harley Crescent, Condell Park, NSW 2200, and in New
Zealand by Transworld Publishers (N.Z.) Ltd., Cnr. Moselle
and Waipareira Avenues, Henderson, Auckland.

Made and printed in Great Britain by
Hunt Barnard Printing Ltd., Aylesbury, Bucks.

Any objection by the visiting team about the ground or the way it is marked out must be made to the Referee before the first kick-off.

Kick-off is a place kick taken from the centre of the half-way line using a recognized kick. The ball must reach the opponents 10m line. If not it shall be kicked again.

When playing a drop-kick a player must allow ball to fall from his hands before kicking it.

Each Touch Judge shall carry a flag to signal his decisions. A Player may not question any signal.

At a Ruck or Maul a Player may not jump on top of other Players.

A Player may not kick any other Player in the teeth.

A mark is awarded when a Player makes a clean catch from a kick, knock-on or throw forward by the other side. The Player must be stationary and shout 'MARK' as ball is caught.

During a match no person other than the Players and Officials may be within the field-of-play unless with permission of the Referee which shall be given only for a special and temporary purpose.

If a Player sees an offence taking place it must be ignored until the Referee blows his whistle. A player may not appeal.

Either a medically trained person or the Referee shall decide as to whether a Player if fit enough to play.

OFF!

Foul play will be dealt with very severely.

13

A Player must when so requested, whether before or during the match, allow the Referee to inspect his dress.

If all fifteen Players and substitutes of one team are sent off or leave the field due to injury, the game shall be awarded to the other side.

No Player shall leave the field unless for a very good reason and only then with the permission of the Referee.

Players may not make a dangerous tackle or tackle with a 'stiff arm'.

Advantage does not apply when the ball, or a Player carrying it, touches the Referee.

Before the ball has been thrown in at a line-out a Player may not use other Players as an aid to jumping for the ball.

A Referee is considered as part of the field-of-play, so play will continue if he is touched by the ball.

Before the ball has been thrown in at a line-out a Player may not make contact with any other Player from either side.

Players will wear regulation clothes at all times during play.

A Player may dig a hole, using his boot to produce a platform on which to put the ball for a place kick.

Any Streaker shall be removed from the field-of-play by the Referee.

A 'Placer' may be used to steady the ball for a penalty kick in adverse weather conditions. The kicker shall decide if one is to be used.

At half-time the teams shall change ends, and there shall be an interval of not more than five minutes when oranges shall be distributed to the Players.

The Referee shall be sole judge as to whether conditions are playable.

A Player must not wear or carry dangerous projections at any time during play.

Deliberate time-wasting is illegal when taking a penalty kick.

A person on the field-of-play must never be tackled if he does not possess the ball.

Smoking is prohibited at all times during a ruck, maul, or a scrummage.

Coaches, Managers, Substitutes or anyone connected with either team shall remain silent whilst play is in progress.

Technical offences shall be punished by a free kick.

A Touch Judge shall clearly show any decision by using his flag (or other suitable object).

When a situation occurs which is beyond the control of the Referee the game shall be stopped.

The biting of players is forbidden and offenders will be punished accordingly.

Players may wear protective clothing providing it is not rigid.

Any objection by either team as regards the number of players in a team may be made at any time but the objection shall not affect any score previously obtained.

The ball when new shall be oval in shape and of four panels. The casing need not be of leather.

If after a tackle the ball carrier is no longer on his feet he is deemed to have been brought to the ground.

It is illegal for any Player to stand on the crossbar of the goal or to use it for his own advantage.

Every Player must have appropriate number displayed on the back of his shirt.

The ball must not be kicked whilst being carried by another Player.

The authority of the Referee will be respected at all times on the field-of-play.

One ball only shall be in use at any one time during the game.

Players must remain silent after a decision by the Referee has been made.

The use of any artificial aids by Players is not permitted under any circumstances.